Whispers between Heartbeats

All rights reserved by Samantha Smedley. All poems are original works and may not be reproduced or sold without express written permission from the author.
Copywrite 2025 Samantha Smedley

Dedicated to all those who want to write. Take the leap of faith, put that pen to paper or type those words. Someone, somewhere will appreciate what you have to say.

When the *heart* first spoke

Chapter One

These poems come from the voice of my younger self — a heart unguarded, discovering its own rhythm for the first time. They hold the rawness of first love, the weight of early sorrow, and the fragile wonder of beginnings. Every word is a pulse of innocence, a whisper before the world taught me how to listen.

Girl in the Mirror

When I look in the mirror, I see a girl who's hurt and torn.
With a heart that is dying because it is worn.
Her face shows no emotion for her feelings are all mixed.
Although you may think so, this can't be easily fixed.
And then a single tear runs down her pallor face.
It leaves her eye so slowly but does not leave a trace.
This face of no emotion now shows a life falling apart.
These feelings that I see are projected from her heart.
She falls down on her knees because she thinks she can't survive.
Forgetting that it's a blessing just to be alive.
The girl in the mirror is a familiar sight to see,
I take a closer look and I realise that the girl in the mirror is me

The Popular Girl

You walk around the school with your mobile phone and toys.
Trying to get attention from the older teenage boys.
You try to be noticed and show that you are best.
By sucking in your tummy and sticking out your chest.
You stroll around the school, with a stick shoved up your ass.
You turn away from everyone as if they're lower class.
Your popular I get it but that doesn't give you the right.
To blow off your friends after a stupid little fight.
So if that's how you're going to be, if that's how you're going to act.
I won't even bother to try and get you back.
I guess I have to accept it, that now you're gone for good.
I didn't want to have to, but now I guess I should.

You used to be the nicest, with your hair all neat and curled.
But now I must realise, that you're just a popular girl.

What You Gunna Do?

You talk about other girls as if I'm not there.
You hide your feelings from me, when I ask for you to share.
I try to figure out where I stand, but I don't seem to see.
Why do I feel inferior? They should be fearing me.
I'm sick of listening bout other girls, it's getting to be too tough.
I'm gunna scream out loud, coz I've really had enough.
So tell me your decision, I've let you think it through.
It's time to ask the question.. "What you gunna do?

Paid my Dues

I put up with your crap and the way you treated me.
I didn't want to believe it, I wouldn't let it be.
You pushed me around and told me what to do.
I didn't want to see it, I couldn't let it be true.
But over time I guess it became real.
That you didn't really care for how I feel.
So I've had enough. I'm leaving you.
It's time to remember I've paid my dues.

One Upon a Time

Once upon a time I really cared.
Once upon a time I wish you would share.
Once upon a time I thought you loved me.
Once upon a time I thought we were meant to be.
Once upon a time I dreamed about you.
Once upon a time you helped me get through.
Once upon a time I hugged you tight.
Once upon a time I thought about you day and night.
But now I see that this once upon a time.
Was nothing but a stupid fairy tale rhyme.

I think I'm in Love

When I first looked into your eyes, the world around me stopped.
I thought it was just a cheap disguise, but now I know it's not.
Every minute of every day I sit and think of you.
And I'd always hope that you would be thinking of me too.
My feelings for you grow every single day.
I can't help it if I feel this way.
Coz I need you and I'll never let you go.
My one and only I love you so

Dealing with deception

There's a little voice inside my head, that's telling me to run.
It says that I have been deceived by my desire for fun.
I can't, I won't believe it, tell me it's not true.
Tell me that I haven't been deceived, say it wasn't you.
I don't believe it, it doesn't seem quite right.
Was is all just a lie when you used to hold me tight.
Were all those kisses just for fun or did you feel a spark.
Did you lie when you told me, I had a special place in your heart.
When you said you love me, did you say it just to score.
Is that all that there is or did you lie about more.
How could I have missed it; with all the signs you made.
You covered my eyes by being sweet, whilst with my heart you played.

You kissed me you hugged me, looked at me with your hypnotic eyes.
But for some unknown reason, I could never you despise.
You've got this hold on me, which I can't break free from.
I can't see what it is, but I know something is wrong.
Although I know the truth now, I can't seem to let you go.
So I will sit here in my silence with all the things I know.

Tell Me

There are three words I want to tell you.
And I'm hoping you will say them too.
But I'm scared that if I reveal my heart.
That we might soon drift apart.
You say don't write letters coz it's gutless and immature.
But it's the only way to you, my feelings that are pure.
So I won't write letters to show you how I feel.
But ask yourself, can our love be real.
I'm not the kind of person who can be played.
There are things that I need to say.
I want to say that I love you.
But I wonder will you say it too?

True Colours

I look at your face and I see your mind.
I look at your smile and I see that your kind.
Sometimes I sit and watch you from afar.
This gives me a chance to see who you are.
Then I look deep into your eyes.
And I find all the feelings that you disguise.
I know that you see me looking at you.
Coz sometimes I see you watching me too.
You look at me with eyes of care.
As if there is something you want to share.
Someday you'll tell me, this i know.
It might not be today, but it could be tomorrow.
And then one day just maybe when i look into your eyes.
You'll tell me your secret, these feelings you disguise.

I miss you

With every breath that i take and every beat of my heart, i find myself missing you.
For each time that i blink and every muscle that i have in the whole of my body i feel myself missing you.
For every jour and minute and second that i am alive since the moment I met you, I am yearning for you, needing just to hear your voice to know you are alright and to tell you that I miss you.
For all the tears I've shed, both happy and sad, for all the memories I have made, I remind myself why I miss you.
So as i sit here and close my eyes i remember the feel of your lips when we kiss and the touch of your skin against mine.
I visualize the moments we've spent together, holding hands as we walk along the river in the afternoon sun, realising its moment like this that make life worth living to the fullest

I cherish each and every moment that we have together, but remember when we are apart I can't help but remember all the things that make life so amazing and remind me that I miss you.

Losses

Have you ever lost someone close to you, they may have died.
It hurts so much that all you want to do is cry.
They may have left for some petty little thing a stupid little fight.
But now you wish they'd just come back so you could make it right.
It hurts so much to realize that you made them go away.
You didn't mean to push them, all you wanted was for them to stay.
But now it's too late they've gone and walked right away from you.
And even though you tried your best there was nothing you could do.

Let Go

My friends told me that i should let you go.
That we should break up, move on and so.
But I can't because without you ,y life is worth naught.
Because life without love is no life at all.
If we were to split up my heart would break in two.
And yet i wonder how this affects you.
My friends only want what is best for me.
I guess I'm not seeing the things that they see.
Maybe I should listen and just let you go.
And forget the feelings that once were so.
But I'll stay only if you promise me.
That we were indefinately meant to be.

Forgive and Forget

You asked me to forgive you, to forget the things you said.
You told me it wasn't true and empty it out of my head.
You said we should just be friends, coz you found another girl.
I wish I could forgive you, but you shattered my whole world.
I hardest thing is that no matter what i say.
I can't get you out of my mind, i think about you night and day.
Why do I let you hurt me, this I do not know.
I guess it's because I honestly love you so.

How can I forget

How can I forget the good times that we shared.
How can I forget that you told me you really cared.
How can I forget you held me in your arms.
How can I forget that you used your charms.
How can I forget that you held me tight.
How can I forget that you used to hold me tight.
So even though it's over and even though your gone.
the memory of you will always live on.

One day, someday, maybe.

One day maybe when you ask for a hug, you'll feel the things that I do when I'm wrapped in your arms.
One day when you come to into my room in the early hours of the morning you will see me and your heart will race.
Maybe one day when you kiss me, you will have to resist the urge to never stop.
Maybe someday when you are telling people about our friendship, you'll realize that I was the one you wanted all along.
Maybe someday you'll look at me and see that all these years everything I've done was for you.
Maybe one day you can love me like I have always loved you.
Maybe one day, someday maybe.

When the *heart* learned to listen

Chapter Two

These poems belong to the older me — a heart tempered by time, softened by reflection, and strengthened by loss and love. They are quieter, deeper beats: the pauses between, the echoes that stay long after the sound fades. Here, the heart does not rush to speak but leans into silence, finding meaning in what was once overlooked.

The ways you love me

Forehead kisses and hugs so tight.
Long conversations and your cuddles at night .
The smiles you give me when you catch me looking at you.
The air blown kisses and whispered I love You's.
Holding hands when we go out.
Or your hand on my leg when we're driving about .
Doing what we do when we are together.
Cooking, cleaning, gaming... whatever
The way you smile when I walk in the door .
Or how you'll sit with me when I'm crying on the floor.
I love all the ways you love me, love what you do.
I love that we found our way back and I love you.

By the time

By the time he realised he wanted to try,
I'd realised I was done.
By the time he decided he shouldn't have left.
I'd realised him leaving was exactly what needed to happen.
By the time he wanted to apologise,
The clouds had cleared and I could see him for who he really was.
By the time he said he would always love me.
I'd realised that it wasn't what love should be.
By the time he wanted to try and blame it all on me.
I'd found my voice and refused to give up without a fight.
By the time he realised it was really over.
I had taken control of my life and moved on.
In the moment it hurt, I felt like I could die.
But by the time it was over.
I'd realised I was stronger than I knew,
and braver than I thought I could ever be.

There will be a day

There will be a day when
I can't pick up the phone and call you.
There will be a day when
You wont be able to give me advice.
There will be a day when
You will we will no longer play pranks on each other.
There will be a day when
You beating us at the clinker game is a think of the past.
There will be a day when
We can't annoy you anymore with the 500 miles song.
There will be a day when
The big bear hugs are no more.
There will be a day when
You can no longer tell me how proud you are of me.
There will be a day when
The photos and memories are all i have left.
One day, some day.
there will be a day
And that day will break my heart.

I have

I have cried Tears of hurt.
tears of loneliness and tears of heartache I have fought.
Fought for my house.
fought to clear my debts and fought to get my name back.
I have held back.
Held back all the words I wanted to say.
held back my tears until I was alone and held back my emotions.
I have been broken.
Broken down by people over and over.
broken by people who I was meant to be able to trust.
I have trusted,
Trusted people I shouldn't,
trusted people who didn't deserve it and trusted instincts.
I have given.
Given my time, my energy and pieces of myself away.
I have cried, fought, held back, been broken.
Trusted and given.
And I have won.

The silence

There's noises in the street children playing ball and laughing,
But the silence is still there.
The tv is on, one of my favourite shows,
But the silence is still there.
My phone beeps with a message from a loved one,
But the silence is still there.
The cats are running about house,
But the silence is still there.
Cars driving around and an ice cream van goes by,
But the silence is still there.
The night time brings the ultimate silence,
The silence is so loud
I can barely hear my thoughts.
It goes on forever with no sign of an end
With the morning sun other noises become clear
But... the silence is still there.

All Ours

The days when we are apart.
And the nights we have together.
When you reach back to hold my hand.
And when you lean in to kiss me.
When you hold me in your arms.
And when you call me your princess.
In all these moments I love you.
And in every other moment as well.
You make the bad moments seem less.
And the happy moments more.
You make me believe that love is possible.
And you make my heart skip .
This kind of love is what I always dreamed of.
And this love is all ours.

To grandad with love

It's hard to keep smiling, especially today.
Because it's been a year since you were taken away.
Your absence leaves a hole bigger then I knew.
Each and every day my heart still misses you.
I didn't get the chance to say my goodbye .
And every time I think of you, I try hard not to cry .
Thank you for all the memories, the love and laughter too.
You're my extraordinary Grandad and I'll always love you.

All I have left

When all I have left are the little moments captured on the screen.
The pictures we took and the pictures we've seen.
The voices recorded in moments we had.
Conversations, laughter and moments so sad.
The memories of you will always be there.
We will never forget and always will share.
When all I have left are the pictures and recordings of you.
When moments feel so hard and I don't know what to do,
I will cherish the lifetime we got to share,
The last memories we made as you sat in your chair.
I will cry oh I will cry, some tears happy some bad.
But I will always remember the memories we had,
Because it's all I have left now no more memories with you to be made.

Because it's all I have left now no more memories with you to be made.
And I will keep them all close, I'll never let them fade.
I miss you oh how I miss you, I keep wanting to call.
But memories are what in have left and my love for you that is all.

From The Ashes

You lit a fire beneath me.
And kept me in the flames.
You took all help from around me,
And you degraded me with names.
You made me think it was normal,
That your behaviour and anger was just.
You confused me with your actions,
By constantly giving and taking away
your trust.
You took pieces of me
And slowly you burnt others away,
You kept threatening to leave,
Then you expected me to be grateful
you chose to stay.
You pushed and pushed the boundaries,
Then complained when I pushed back.
Every opinion I had,
Made you go on the attack.
Nothing I did was good enough,
Nothing I did was right.
And everything you said,
Made me lay away at night.

Questioning your motives,
Questioning what I thought I knew.
Making me doubt,
All the things I thought I knew.
But through all this,
Through all the pain.
I've risen from the ashes,
To reclaim.
My life, my home, my family,
And all you tried to take.
You tried to burn me in the fire,
But I did not ever break.
Instead I rise from the ashes,
The flames melted the pain away.
And I stand strong and whole,
Ready to take on every new day.

It's Me, Not You

You lied, but it was my fault.
You lost your temper and put holes in the door and marks on the walls, but it was my fault.
You used me as an excuse to not have to go events or family dinners, but it was my fault.
You spent all your money on games and junk food and had no fuel to get to work, but it was my fault.
You couldn't be bothered to clean your own mess, but it was my fault.
You wouldn't put in any effort for anything, but it was my fault.
You didn't care to remember anything important, but it was my fault.
You put me down, told me I was worthless, but it was my fault.
You left and it was again my fault.

I Hope

I hope one day you understand how many people you've hurt.
I hope that all you've put out into this world comes back to you.
I hope one day you get exactly what you deserve.
I hope that one day you will reflect and make the change.
I hope you come to realize that life wasn't as bad as you made it out to be.
That people really did care about you.
That despite how you treated us, we stayed.
I hope that some day you can be truly happy.
That you can appreciate what you have.
And I hope that one day you can make this world a better place then you found it.

I Miss You

I miss you in the morning,
I wake up and think about you.
I miss you in the day,
I want to call you and hear your voice.
I miss you when I use the bowl you gave me,
You said it would remind me of you. (It does).
I miss you when I wear too much black,
And I hear your voice in my head, telling me to wear more colour.
I miss you when I make, eat or smell Mock Chicken.
I miss you when I see photos or notes you've written,
Or the trinkets you've bought me.
I miss you when I get in the car and I go to call you,
But then I remember you won't answer anymore.
I miss you when I see magpies,
Remembering how you used to feed them in the backyard each night.

Let's face it , I miss you all the time,
I still cry, I wish I had done more.
You are always loved Grandma,
And now you are back with Grandad,
And we miss you both.

The Forgotten One

The one who never gets the call back.
The one whose plans always get changed or cancelled.
The one who will sit and wait for invitations to arrive.
The one who will leave their phone on loud just in case you need them.
The one that when you look back has always been there through all the highs and lows.
The one you always forget about.
The one who remembers your birthday, or anniversary and never complains when you forget theirs.
Who despite you forgetting to call back, answers you on the first ring.
The one who you cancelled plans with all the time regardless of reason, who will still go out of their way for you.
The one who despite feeling like they are constantly overlooked, will smile and pretend like no time has passed.

Who will smile and wave and play the good friend, daughter, sister, wife, mother – whatever role she is required to play. The forgotten one.

My Own Insecurities

There will always be the feeling that I am not good enough.
That at any moment you'll find someone you want more then me.
That I am just a place holder until something better comes along.
I will always feel like I am not pretty enough, smart enough or whole enough.
The feeling that the past Is going to come back and bite me in the ass again lingers.
I will always be scared that one day I will wake up, all the good that has happened will be gone.
My insecurities linger, but you make them silent for a little.
You make me feel loved and appreciated, but in the quiet they start to return.

The Ones you Choose.

The Sister, unrelated who is there through it all.
The little Brother who will laugh at you but pick you up when you fall.
The Mother who loves you like you are her own.
The aunts and the uncles who aren't your blood but welcome you in their home.
Those people who support you, love you and care.
The people who remind you they will always be there.
Nieces and nephews, you've claimed and love as if related to you.
The ones you love like blood, who help you get through.
Never asking for anything, no cost for that affection.
Only offering love, kindness and protection.
The Friends, The Family, the ones you choose.

Ode to the Step Mum

You love them like they're yours, you take the good with the bad.
You are there to comfort, explain and give answers to their but whys.
You wipe noses, wash clothes, make sure they eat and drink.
You plan activities, sort toys and think if all the things they need.
You smile when they come to you and you listen when they speak.
You lay with them at night time when they can't get to sleep.
You buy clothes for them when they need it and pack lunches and snacks.
And you've got the tissues, band aids, cream and medicine at the ready.
You didn't birth them, but you love and support them.
And you are ok being the bad person when they need tough love.
You never want to replace their mum, but you will always be another safe space for them.

.

You make your house into their second home and do everything to make sure they belong.
And when they go you miss them, despite the arguments and button pushing.
You miss their hugs, their smiles and their laughs.
There is no guidebook to help you navigate this role. Just a bunch of unwritten rules and common courtesies as you walk the fine line of a bonus mum.
It's not a job for everyone to be able to love someone else's child like you would love your own.
But its a job that many women take on happily.
To all those who love and care for children that aren't their own flesh and blood.
Keep going, it isn't always easy but oh my God it's amazing.

www.ingramcontent.com/pod-product-compliance
Lightning Source LLC
Chambersburg PA
CBHW072022290426
44109CB00018B/2313